EVERYDAY HEROES
Take A Stand

By Jill C. Wheeler

Published by Abdo & Daughters, 4940 Viking Drive, Suite 622, Edina, Minnesota 55435.

Copyright © 1996 by Abdo Consulting Group, Inc., Pentagon Tower, P.O. Box 36036, Minneapolis, Minnesota 55435 USA. International copyrights reserved in all countries. No part of this book may be reproduced in any form without written permission from the publisher.

Printed in the United States.

Edited by Julie Berg

Library of Congress Cataloging-in-Publication Data
Wheeler, Jill C., 1964-
   Everyday Heroes Take a Stand / Jill C. Wheeler
    p. cm. -- (Everyday Heroes)
   Includes index.
   Summary: Profiles the lives of young people who saw something that needed to be done and did it; includes suggestions on how anyone can take a stand.
    ISBN 1-56239-702-8
   1. Heroes--Biography--Juvenile literature. [1. Heroes.] I. Title.
CT107.W615 1996   96-7599
920'.009'04--dc20   CIP
[B]   AC

Contents

Turning Beliefs Into Action

It's one thing to see something you believe needs to be changed. It's another matter to do something about it. Yet throughout history, there have been people who did more than simply see a problem. They decided to take a stand.

Some of them have been young people just like you. One was Frenchman Louis Braille. He lived in the 1800s. Braille was only three years old when an accident left him blind. As a student, he couldn't read like the other children. He decided to create a way for blind people to read. By the time he was 15 years old, he had created the Braille method of reading. Braille uses bumps for letters. Blind people around the world can read, thanks to this young man's work.

Another was Frederick Douglass. Douglass grew up an African-American slave in Maryland in the 1800s. When he was 12 years old, he overheard his owners say slaves shouldn't learn to read or write. The owners said knowing those skills would help slaves escape. Douglass learned to read and write anyway. He studied speeches and laws. When he was 20, he escaped from slavery. He became a powerful voice in the movement to free all slaves.

More recently, Ryan White made headlines by taking a stand to help people with AIDS. AIDS is the fatal disease Acquired Immune Deficiency Syndrome. The Indiana boy contracted AIDS from a blood transfusion when he was just 12 years old. He spent the rest of his life fighting discrimination against people with AIDS. He died from the disease in 1990.

There are young people like that alive today, too. People like Ellen Bigger, who started the drug-prevention program "Drug-Free Homes" when she was a teenager. Or people like Trevor Ferrell, who began helping the homeless in his hometown of Philadelphia when he was just 11. Trevor began by handing out blankets to homeless people. His work has grown into a non-profit organization with several homeless shelters and related programs.

There are similar heroes taking a stand today. Following are profiles of a few of them. They are stories of young people who saw something that needed to be done and did it. In the final chapter, you'll find out how you can take a stand, too.

William Marin thought the officials in his hometown of Riverside, California could do a better job of addressing issues affecting youth. It would help, he thought, if they could think like kids. It would be even better if they would listen to real kids.

That's why in 1992, he sent a letter to the mayor of Riverside. In his letter, he suggested the city create a Youth Advisory Council. "There are a lot of issues in government," William says. "Officials don't always have the necessary insights to address them. Then when they try to address them, they don't always do a good job. I wanted a Youth Council to advise the city on issues like violence, drugs and gangs. They're things young people see each day when they go to school."

City officials agreed with William. They thought the government might be able to prevent such problems if officials had more input from young people. Plus, William's timing couldn't have been better. Just months before, rioting had rocked nearby Los Angeles.

For the next two years, William worked toward his dream. He circulated petitions for a Youth Council at high schools in Riverside County. He talked to hundreds of students. He attended public hearings. He worked with city commissions.

Sometimes the efforts made him frustrated. "Things work slowly in city government," he says. "It's a challenge. There are meeting rules that say you can't talk about anything that's not on the agenda. There's lots of red tape

In 1994, William became the first council chair for the Riverside, California Youth Advisory Council.

and it's hard to work with everyone's schedule." Yet William persisted and in January 1994, his dream came true. The city created a Youth Council. City officials chose William as the first council chair.

William's efforts gained him the 1993 Young American Medal from the United States Department of Justice. He met with United States Attorney General Janet Reno and President Bill Clinton.

William remains active in government. He has served on five government boards. One was the Juvenile Justice & Delinquency Prevention Commission. As a part of his work, he visits juvenile detention facilities. "I like to talk with the kids there to get a feel for what they're going through," he says. "It's been enriching to ask questions.

I find out about people's lives. It lets me go beyond what people think superficially. It's allowed me to see the challenges they face."

He also belongs to a community service club. The club's projects include the Adopt-A-Street program. The program helps keep the community clean. The club also helps feed homeless people.

After college, William plans to go into government work. His dream is to be elected to Congress. He realizes that's a tough job, but he's never let hard work stop him before. "I've always tried hard," he says. "I believe that through hard work, you can accomplish whatever you seek to do."

"You can accomplish whatever you seek to do."

Lenti Smith

Lenti Smith refused to believe it when people said kids were getting worse. "All my life I've heard grownups talking about how kids today don't care about the future," she said. "I decided I wanted to make a difference. I was sure there were other kids who felt the same way."

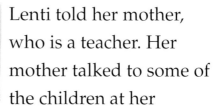

Lenti told her mother, who is a teacher. Her mother talked to some of the children at her school about Lenti's plan. They agreed it would be a good idea. The word spread quickly. Many kids said they wanted to help, too.

In 1990, Lenti started an organization in her hometown of Lebanon, Tennessee. She named it YOUTH.

YOUTH stands for Youth Organization Unites to Help. YOUTH members get involved in helping other people both in and beyond their communities.

Since then, YOUTH has grown to more than 200 members. Some members are as young as kindergarten students. Some are as old as freshmen or sophomores in high school. All have a single goal: to help other people.

YOUTH members around Lebanon now are working to adopt several children in developing countries. They are holding fund-raisers to make money. The money will help their adopted kids get food, clothing, and an education. YOUTH members also are raising money for another project. They want to help Lebanon build a community playhouse.

Lenti Smith meeting Barbara Bush in 1993, after receiving the Maxwell House Real Hero Award.

Lenti says it hasn't been hard to get young people excited about making a difference. She says what can be hard is deciding what to do. "We get a lot of letters from groups that want our help," she says. "We just have to take it one day at a time and do what we can do."

Lenti's efforts have not gone unnoticed. In 1993, Maxwell House named her a Real Hero. She and her family flew to Washington, D.C., to meet former first lady Barbara Bush. She also received the Weekly Reader's Jefferson Award in 1991.

Lenti hopes other children will start YOUTH chapters in their own cities. She also encourages kids not to give up on making a difference. "Kids shouldn't believe

everything they hear," she says. "There are other kids out there that want to help. If they think they can't make a difference, they're wrong."

After school, Lenti plans to go to college and become a lawyer. She also hopes that YOUTH will one day be a national organization.

If you would like to start a YOUTH chapter in your hometown, Lenti wants to hear from you. You can write to her at: Lenti Smith, 307 Blair Lane, Lebanon, Tennessee, 37087.

"Take it one day at a time and do what we can do."

If there's a disaster nearby, chances are Navin Narayan will be there to lend a hand. The Fort Worth, Texas teen has taught thousands of people what to do in case of an emergency. He's helped countless others himself.

Navin's passion for helping others began when he was in ninth grade. He needed to complete 60 hours of community service work for his school. He decided to volunteer with the American Red Cross.

Navin has done many things with the Red Cross. He's taught CPR and First Aid. He's been on call 24 hours a day as a Disaster Services Volunteer. He's arranged housing for families left homeless by storms. He's even helped find critical medicines for fire victims in the middle of the night.

Navin's work earned him a special honor. The Red Cross picked him to be the National Youth Speaker at their annual convention. He also became a member of the Red Cross's National Youth Advisory Committee on Youth Involvement.

Just before the convention, Navin faced a crisis in his own life. Doctors diagnosed him with a rare form of cancer. They told him there was a 50-50 chance of survival. They began giving him radiation and chemotherapy treatments. He spent almost half of his time in the hospital for almost two years.

Throughout the ordeal, Navin remembered what he'd said at the convention. "Life is a path," he told the people. "Sometimes it's a tough path. It's important not to look too far down the path. Otherwise, you won't see what's happening in your life right now."

Eventually Navin recovered from his illness. Now he is attending Harvard University. He continues to work with the Red Cross youth committee. His goal is to help people in developing countries.

Navin said his illness changed his outlook on life. "I used to volunteer to show off," he said. "Sometimes it takes

that for people to do good things. Now I can empathize with people who are suffering. I know how important it is to have health and peace of mind. I want to help others have those things, too."

"Life is a path. Sometimes it's a tough path."

Dorion Simmons

Don't tell Dorion Simmons that inner city kids don't have a chance in the business world. He's working to make sure they do.

Dorion is one of just four young people on the national leadership team of a special program. The program is called WAVE. It stands for Work Achievement Values in Education. WAVE helps teachers prepare inner city youth for the world of work.

Dorion and WAVE work with at-risk young people. These are kids who grow up surrounded by problems like poverty, drugs, gangs and violence. People thought Dorion himself was at risk.

His mother died when he was just two years old. His father lived in another state. He was raised by his grandfather, who was a long-distance trucker. He often saw violence and gangs while he was growing up.

Dorion didn't give in to the temptation of drugs, gangs, and violence. When he was a sophomore in high school, he took a unique summer job. Part of the day he worked. The rest of the day he went to school. At the school, he learned about the WAVE class.

WAVE teaches students how to get and hold a job. They learn how to fill out a job application. They learn how to increase their vocabulary. They learn basic math skills. "The classes are more interesting than regular school,"

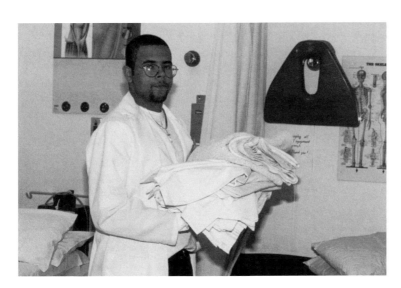

Dorion landed a job as a physical therapy aide at a hospital near Chicago.

Dorion says. "You're learning something you can use now." Students who dropped out of high school also can study to get their GED. A GED is like a high school diploma.

Dorion graduated from high school in 1994. He landed a job as a physical therapy aide at a hospital near Chicago. He credits WAVE for helping. "When I applied at the hospital, they were so impressed with the application they hired me right away," he said. "WAVE has helped other kids apply for jobs by giving them confidence."

Dorion often talks to young people at retreats and seminars. "I like to talk to young people about leadership skills and help them if they're not doing well," he said. "Lots of times they don't feel comfortable talking with their teachers, but I'm more their age."

He also reminds them that where they grow up doesn't have to determine their future. "Just because you're not in the best neighborhood doesn't mean you have to do what other people are doing," he said. "Lots of kids feel they need to go with the crowd. But everyone needs to know what's right and wrong for himself. Everyone needs to look out for his own future."

As for his future, Dorion plans to stay involved with WAVE and helping kids. He also is attending the College of Lake County near Chicago to become a physical therapist.

"Everyone needs to look out for his own future."

Paola Pagnanelli & Cindy Loy

Chicago's Amundsen High School coach, Jim Gemskie, planned special field trips for some of his students. He wanted to take them to a place where they wouldn't want to be.

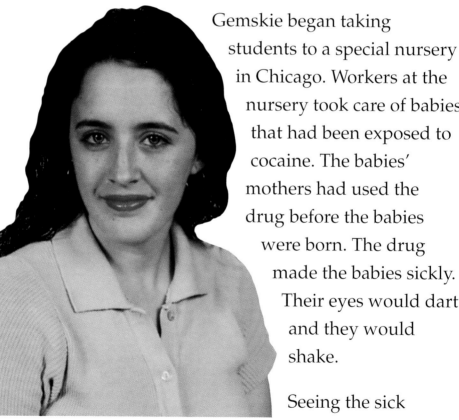

Paola Pagnanelli

Gemskie began taking students to a special nursery in Chicago. Workers at the nursery took care of babies that had been exposed to cocaine. The babies' mothers had used the drug before the babies were born. The drug made the babies sickly. Their eyes would dart and they would shake.

Seeing the sick babies moved many of the students.

Some decided to do something about it. They wanted to help the nursery take care of the babies. In 1992, they held a "Kids Helping Kids" Walk-A-Thon to raise money for the cocaine baby unit.

Four years later, the Walk-A-Thon is a much bigger event. Amundsen High School students Paola Pagnanelli and Cindy Loy are part of a planning committee for the event. They work to make sure the Walk-A-Thon continues to be a success.

"Each year our goal gets bigger," says Paola, the top Walk-A-Thon fund-raiser in 1995. "We're getting more and more students involved and making more money for the nursery. Last year, we had 3,500 students and raised $100,000."

Adds Cindy, "We're shooting for 7,000 students in 1996. We hope to have 125 schools involved."

Cindy and Paola put in many hours preparing for the Walk-A-Thon. They work with a committee to find corporate sponsors to donate money and other supplies. They sign up students to gather pledges and walk in the event. They arrange for prizes for the students who raise the most money. The nursery uses the money from the Walk-A-Thon to buy supplies. They buy items like diapers, formula and baby monitors.

Both students have received awards for their work with the nursery. Yet even without the honors, they say the extra time and effort is worthwhile. "You need to treat other people like you'd like to be treated," says Paola. "If it were me, I'd want someone to help me."

"My parents taught me to help those who need it," adds Cindy. "God's blessed my family a tremendous amount. It's only fair that we give back to people who don't have as much as we do."

Cindy Loy

"Some people bug you about being a goody two shoes when you try to help," Cindy says. "My challenge is winning them over. You can do a lot of fun things and still be involved in helping others."

Paola, who is from Argentina originally, plans to go to college and major in business and politics. She wants to get involved in community service after graduation. Cindy, who is from Guatemala, hopes to go to college to become a doctor. Her goal is to work in an inner city Chicago hospital.

"You need to treat other people like you'd like to be treated."

How To Be A Hero

You, too, can turn your beliefs into action. You need to be persistent. You need to know when to ask for help. You also need to encourage other people to join you in supporting your cause.

You can take a stand either alone, or by working with others. Often, if people see what you're doing and like it, they'll join you. You may start small. You may also begin a movement.

To get started, list the things in which you deeply believe. To do that, begin by asking yourself these questions:

- What things are happening in the world that I feel are good? What things should there be more of?
- What things are happening in the world that I feel are wrong? What things would I like to change?
- If I could change just one thing in the world, what would it be?
- What would I have to do to make that change happen?

Once you know the issue you want to address, you can get started. The first step is to learn all you can about it. Begin by going to your local library. Look for books and magazines that address that issue. What work already is being done to help? What organizations or individuals are working on the problem?

Then, think about what needs to be done. Sometimes, problems seem too big to do anything about. In that case, break them down. If you're concerned that people around the world are hungry, focus on the hungry people in your hometown. What can you do to help them? Begin on the local level and work your way up.

Think about different ways of helping, too. Maybe you're concerned about certain things a company is doing. If you disagree with them, write them a letter and tell them why. Have your friends write, too. A group of young people wrote letters to McDonald's restaurants. They asked McDonald's to stop using foam shells to package their sandwiches. They felt the shells were causing pollution. Eventually, McDonald's switched to paper wrappings on sandwiches.

Perhaps a new law can address your concern. Ask yourself what level of government needs to be involved. Would a new rule in your city solve the problem? Then write to city officials. Does it need to be a new law around the country? Then write to your representatives in Congress. Get your family and friends to write, too.

Maybe people just need to know more about it so they can change the way they act. You can help educate them. After all, you've researched the issue already. To help them learn, talk to your family and friends. Write letters to the editor of your local newspaper. Write up a flyer and pass it around. Inform people of the importance of your issue. Most of all, tell them what they can do about it, too.

If you'd like more information on taking a stand, check out the book, *The Kid's Guide to Social Action* by Barbara A. Lewis (Free Spirit Publishing.) It's a step-by-step guide to making a difference on a wide range of problems.

Remember, taking a stand can be a worthwhile project. Plus, you might even have some fun along the way.

GLOSSARY OF TERMS

AIDS — a fatal disease that can be spread through blood.

braille — a system of reading and writing that uses raised dots to represent letters.

CPR (cardiopulmonary resuscitation) — a method of helping people breathe again once they've stopped.

chemotherapy — using special chemicals to treat a disease, such as cancer.

discrimination — to favor one person over another for no good reason.

juvenile detention facility — a place where young people are sent when they break the law.

petition — a written request for something that includes signatures of people who support it.

physical therapy — a branch of medicine that helps people heal through physical and mechanical treatments like exercise.

radiation — using special waves to treat certain diseases, such as cancer.

red tape — official procedures that are complicated and slow.

transfusion — to transfer something, such as blood, from one person to another.

Index